HAVENLIGHT

Published by HavenLight, 380 E 620 S Suite B, American Fork, UT 84003
801.763.7956   1.800.366.2781

Gifts
from Heaven

by Liz Lemon Swindle

God gave us the gift of His only begotten Son.

She shall bring forth a son, and they shall call his name Jesus. ~ Matt 1:23

Jesus gave us the gift of family.

Children, obey your parents in all things: for this is well pleasing unto the Lord.
~ *Colossians 3:20*

$\mathcal{J}$esus gave us the gift of love.

A new commandment I give unto you, that ye love one another as I have loved you.
~ John 13:34

Jesus gave us the gift of prayer.

After this manner therefore pray ye: Our Father which art in heaven, Hallowed be thy name. Thy kingdom come. Thy will be done in earth, as it is in heaven. ~ *Matthew 6:9-10*

$\mathcal{J}$esus gave us the gift of faith.

And immediately Jesus stretched forth his hand, and caught him, and said unto him, O thou of little faith, wherefore didst thou doubt? ~ *Matthew 14:31*

*J*esus gave us the gift of healing.

And Jesus went about...healing every sickness
and every disease among the people.
~ *Matthew 9:35*

$\mathcal{J}$esus gave us the gift of agency.

Choose you this day whom ye will serve; but as for me and my house, we will serve the Lord.

~ Joshua 24:15

Jesus gave us the gift of hope.

Jesus answered and said unto her, Whosoever drinketh of this water shall thirst again: But whosoever drinketh of the water that I shall give him shall never thirst.

~ John 4:13-14

Jesus gave us the gift of peace.

Peace I leave with you, my peace I give unto you.
~ John 14:27

*J*esus gave us the gift of gratitude.

And one of them, when he saw that he was healed, turned back, and with a loud voice glorified God.
~ Luke 17:15

$\mathcal{J}$esus
gave us
the gift
of joy.

*Yet I will rejoice in the Lord, I will
joy in the God of my salvation.*
~ Habakkuk 3:18

Always remember God's greatest gift, His Son.

For God so loved the world, that he gave his only begotten Son, that whosoever believeth in him should not perish, but have everlasting life.

~ John 3:16